Penny Farthing
goes to school
TO TEACH ROAD SAFETY

Author
Wendy Roberts
Illustrator
Amy Bradley

AuthorHouse™ UK Ltd.
500 Avebury Boulevard
Central Milton Keynes, MK9 2BE
www.authorhouse.co.uk
Phone: 08001974150

First published by AuthorHouse 09/30/2011
ISBN: 978-1-4490-9700-4 (sc)

Printed in the United States of America

This book is printed on acid-free paper.

authorHOUSE®

Penny helps her children, Rose and Anne, get ready for school.

They have their breakfast and then they all walk to school together.

Penny drops her children off at school, she continues to walk the rest of her journey to the nearby police station.

Penny is a police officer called Police Constable Penny Farthing.

Penny walks the beat, she drives a police car and rides a police mountain bike.

Penny arrives at the Newtown police station.

Penny has to wear a police uniform. She puts on her cravat, her epaulet and her radio. She then puts on her stab-proof vest which protects her.

Finally, she puts her belt around her waist and clips it into place.

The belt Penny wears has lots of kit upon it. It has a first aid pouch in case anybody is hurt when she is out and about on foot patrol.

Penny also has silver handcuffs which she puts on people if they try to run away from her. She also has a baton to protect herself.

Today, Penny has agreed to talk to the children at Newtown Primary about ROAD SAFETY.

Penny turns on her police radio, and tells the controller on the other end where she is going and she books herself busy there.

Penny is riding her police bicycle to the school.

She is very careful and is wearing her cycle hat, gloves and yellow T-shirt so other road users can clearly see her, especially in bad weather.

When Penny arrives at the school, the children rush over to see her. She shows the children her bike.

While police officer Penny is showing the children the push-bike, a lady can be heard speaking on her police radio.

Samantha says,

"Who is that, speaking on your radio?"

Penny replies, "That is the controller, who sends all the police officers to different kinds of incidents. She is talking to the other police officers. Can you hear her?"

As the controller is talking on the radio,

tHe ScHooL BeLL Sounds

tHe ChilDren RUSH off to Li...

Mrs Smith, the teacher of Class One, comes outside and asks the children to quietly walk into school. Penny walks into the school along with the children and Mrs Smith.

e up, ready TO walk INTO school.

Mrs Smith asks the children to sit quietly, as police officer Penny wan[ts]
to speak to them.

Penny asks the children if they have ever been shown how to cross the
road safely, lots of children put their hands up.

Jasmine puts up her hand and says

" Mummy tells me to hold her hand when i cross the road."

Penny smiles and says

"Yes, that is right, Jasmine. If an adult is with you, you can cross the road safely holding their hand, well done."

"STOP AT A SAFE PLACE TO CROSS THE ROAD, AWAY FROM PARKED CARS, SO YOU CAN CLEARLY SEE ACROSS THE ROAD IN BOTH DIRECTIONS. YOU SHOULD BE STANDING AWAY FROM THE KERB"

"IF IT IS NOT SAFE TO CROSS, THEN YOU MUST NOT CROSS THE ROAD"

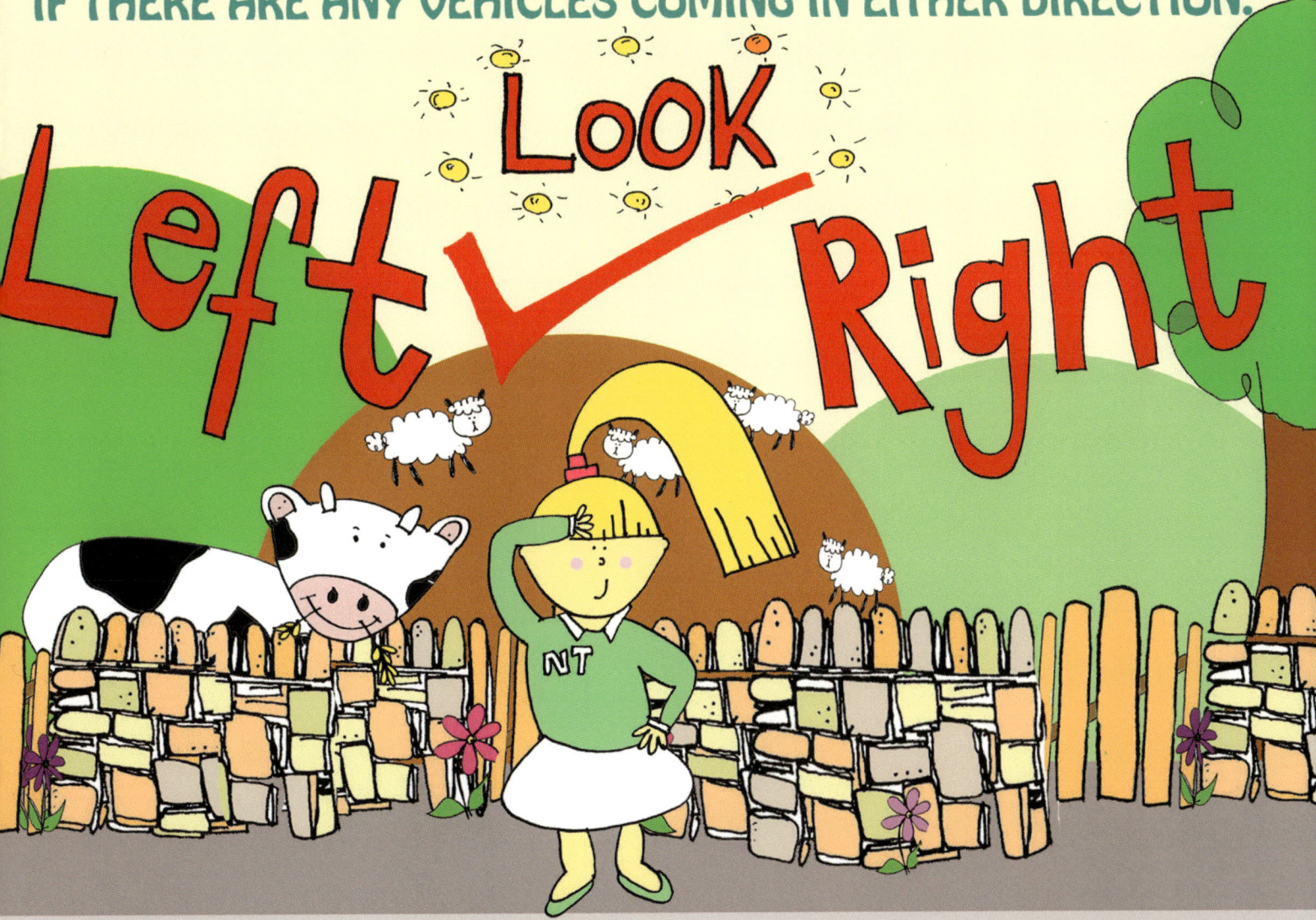

"You must listen for any vehicles coming that you may not be able to see."

Tweet Tweet....

BUZZ BUZZ

flutter flutter

wiggle wiggle

TIP TOE TIP TOE

"If you can hear cars coming you must not cross until it is safe to do so."

Police officer Penny asks the children,

"Shall we go outside in front of the school together and practice crossing the road safely?"

The children of Class One put up their hands eagerly and say yes.

Mrs. Smith along with Penny and the classroom assistant walk with the children to the nearby road outside the school.

The children practice crossing the road with the teachers and Penny.

Penny then says ,

After the children practice crossing the road, they all return to school and invite Penny to join them for their snack. Penny gladly agrees.

Penny enjoys eating her snacks with the children of Class One.

She thanks the children for behaving so well and listening to her.

Penny waves goodbye to the children and rides off on her bike after putting her cycle helmet on.

Penny returns to Newtown police station and puts her bicycle away for the night.

Penny puts her kit away for the night and she says goodnight to the controller on her radio before switching it off and putting it into her locker.

Penny is at work the following day.

She is riding past Newtown primary when she sees one of the mums from the school, whom she recognises. Penny stops on her bike and Jasmine walks up to her with her mummy.

"Last night she was playing in the garden

and her ball went onto the main road."

"I saw Jasmine run out onto the path and thought she was going to run onto the road without looking,

but she didn't. Jasmine STOPPED at the roadside in a safe place,

' I was really surprised! She then carefully walked onto the road, looking and listening all around her, making sure it was still safe to cross.

She then collected her ball and walked back again."

Jasmine's mum continued, saying,

Penny agrees with Jasmine's mummy and says "All children should be taught how to cross the road safely."

Penny gets back on her bicycle,

and Jasmine and her mummy wave goodbye to her. When it is safe to do so Penny looks all around her, while still listening for vehicles and waits for a safe gap in the traffic. She cycles off towards the police station.

Penny returns to the police station, she puts her bike away for the night along with her kit and says goodnight to the controller.

Penny leaves the police station for the night and walks to collect her children from school

they all walk home together.

Lightning Source UK Ltd.
Milton Keynes UK
UKIC03n1410021115
261922UK00004B/24